# In the Fish Tank

Written by Alison Hawes

Illustrated by John and Gus art

**Collins**

Jez has a tank.

3

Jez has a rock.

Jez has a ship.

7

9

# Jez fills the tank.

11

Six fish in the tank.

13

/sh/

14

/nk/

15

# After reading

**Letters and Sounds:** Phase 3

**Word count:** 40

**Focus phonemes:** /nk/ /sh/ /x/ /j/ /z/ /y/

**Common exception words:** the, put, my

**Curriculum links:** Understanding the World: The World

**Early learning goals:** Listening and attention: listen to stories, accurately anticipating key events and respond to what is heard with relevant comments, questions or actions; Understanding: answer 'how' and 'why' questions about experiences and in response to stories or events; Reading: read and understand simple sentences; Use phonic knowledge to decode regular words and read them aloud accurately; Read some common irregular words

## Developing fluency

- Your child may enjoy hearing you read the story.
- Model reading a speech bubble with expression. Now read the book with your child, asking them to read all of the speech bubbles with expression.

## Phonic practice

- Practise reading words that contain new phonemes.
- Say the sounds in the words below.
- Ask your child to repeat the sounds and then say the word.

    p/i/nk    pink          sh/e/ll/s    shells          s/u/nk/e/n    sunken

- Look at the 'I spy sounds' pages (14–15) together. How many words can your child point out that contain the /nk/ sound or the /sh/ sound? (*tank, ink, sink, ship, fish, sheep, shells*)

## Extending vocabulary

- Ask your child if they can tell you an antonym (opposite) for each of the following words:

    out    (*in*)                    fill    (*empty*)

- Now ask your child if they can tell you a synonym for each of the following words:

    rock    (*stone, pebble*)        ship    (*boat*)